212°
LEADERSHIP

THE 10 RULES FOR HIGHLY EFFECTIVE LEADERSHIP

MAC ANDERSON

2

212° **LEADERSHIP**—The 10 Rules for Highly Effective Leadership

Table of Contents

212° LEADERSHIP INTRODUCTION

There's a law of science that could change the way you think about leadership:

> **At 211 degrees, water is hot. At 212 degrees, it boils. With boiling water, comes steam. And steam can power a locomotive.**
> **And... it's that one extra degree that makes all the difference!**

That's what this little book is all about... how that one extra degree of leadership can make the difference not only in your own success... but also in the success of those you lead... and in that of your organization.

I've always been fascinated with the qualities and characteristics of great leaders. History has identified many qualities and characteristics of great leaders, and, of course, no person embodies them all. But the great leaders I've known, or read about have one simple thing in common: *They have developed their leadership styles around their personalities and their values, and in the end, their actions are consistent with what they truly believe.*

212° Leaders have made the leap from good to great. They are able to not only rally the troops to committed, purposeful action, but also to create an environment where quality and innovation are the norm, rather than the exception.

In this book, I've offered 10 rules for 212° Leadership. Hopefully they will make you think … help you grow … and inspire that extra degree of passion to take your leadership skills from effective to extraordinary!

Are you ready to be a 212° Leader?

Mac Anderson
Founder, Simple Truths

CHAPTER 1

THINK
SERVE
... NOT LEAD

→ *"Leaders are leaders because they are the greater servants. The way up is down..."*
— *Francis M. Cosgrove Jr.*

When your employees think of your leadership style, what do they see? Someone focused only on going up the organizational ladder? Or a servant leader ... someone committed to serving both your customers and your employees?

Walt Disney was one of those leaders. ***In How to Be Like Walt,*** author Pat Williams recounts numerous examples of how Walt's servant leadership was just a part of who he was, including this one from actor Dean Jones:

A gardener at the Disney studio left some tools in an empty parking space. When a producer drove up and saw the tools in his space, he honked at the gardener and gave the poor man a chewing out. Walt walked up and interrupted the producer's tirade. "Hold it!" he said. "Don't you ever treat one of my employees like that! This man has been with me longer than you have, so you'd better be good to him!"

That was Walt. To his employees, he was not only a leader. He was their defender and their servant. That's what separates leaders from bosses.

Seeing a true servant leader in action can truly change your life. While I've had the good fortune to meet many successful businesspeople, authors and speakers during my career, I've never met anyone that "walked the talk" more than Ken Blanchard. Over the last 20 years, Ken has probably sold more books than any other business author. His classic, ***The One Minute Manager***, has sold more than 10 million copies. He has also built a large training company with the focus on servant leadership and customer service.

"SERVANT-LEADERSHIP IS ALL
ABOUT MAKING THE GOALS CLEAR
AND THEN ROLLING YOUR SLEEVES UP
AND DOING WHATEVER IT TAKES TO HELP
PEOPLE WIN. IN THAT SITUATION,

THEY DON'T WORK
FOR YOU, YOU WORK
FOR THEM."

— KEN BLANCHARD

"THE GOAL OF MANY LEADERS IS TO GET PEOPLE TO THINK MORE HIGHLY OF THE LEADER. THE GOAL OF A GREAT LEADER IS TO HELP PEOPLE TO THINK HIGHLY OF THEMSELVES."

— J. CARLA NORTCUTT

"THE FIRST RESPONSIBILITY OF A LEADER IS TO DEFINE REALITY. THE LAST IS TO SAY THANK YOU. IN BETWEEN, THE LEADER IS A SERVANT."
— MAX DE PREE

While visiting him at his San Diego office, I learned that one of his employees who worked in the warehouse had recently passed away. Ken had invited the employee's wife to come to his office. When she arrived, he spent an hour walking around with her carrying a tape recorder to record all of the wonderful memories that other employees had of her husband. When the wife left, she said it was a day she'd never forget.

You see, what many leaders would have considered a waste of time, Ken saw as an opportunity to serve and to thank his people. He doesn't do it because it's expected of him; he does it because he truly cares. It comes from the heart, and his people love him for being the servant leader that he is.

Servant leaders are those others want to follow.

In his book, **The Right to Lead,** John C. Maxwell points out that an effective leader is someone others can trust to take them where they want to go.

Here are his guidelines for becoming that type of leader:

➔ Let go of your ego.

The truly great leaders are not in leadership for personal gain. They lead in order to serve other people.

➔ Become a good follower first.

Rare is the effective leader who didn't learn to become a good follower first. That is why a leadership institution such as the United States Military Academy teaches its officers to become effective followers first—and why West Point has produced more leaders than the Harvard Business School.

Build positive relationships.

Leadership is influence, nothing more, nothing less. Today's generation of leaders seem particularly aware of this because title and position mean so little to them. They know intuitively that people go along with people they get along with.

Work with excellence.

No one respects and follows mediocrity. Leaders who earn the right to lead give their all to what they do. They bring into play not only their skills and talents, but also great passion and hard work. They perform on the highest level of which they are capable.

Rely on discipline, not emotion.

Leadership is often easy during the good times. It's when everything seems to be against you—when you're out of energy, and you don't want to lead—that you earn your place as a leader.

➜ Make adding value your goal.

When you look at the leaders whose names are revered long after they have finished leading, you find that they were men and women who helped people to live better lives and reach their potential. That is the highest calling of leadership—and its highest value.

➜ Give your power away.

One of the ironies of leadership is that you become a better leader by sharing whatever power you have, not by saving it all for yourself. If you use your power to empower others, your leadership will extend far beyond your grasp.

"ORGANIZATIONS EXIST TO SERVE. PERIOD. LEADERS LIVE TO SERVE. PERIOD."
— TOM PETERS

"GOOD LEADERS MUST FIRST BECOME GOOD SERVANTS."

— ROBERT K. GREENLEAF

CHAPTER 2

COMPANIES
DON'T
SUCCEED
...PEOPLE DO

 *"Take time to appreciate employees and they will reciprocate in a thousand ways."*
— *Bob Nelson*

As a leader, it's natural to assume that your focus should be on bringing in ... and retaining customers. While that, of course, is the end goal of any business, 212° leaders must change their focus **INTERNALLY** ... to recruiting ... and retaining their best people.

"OUR EMPLOYEES ARE LIKE EXTENDED MEMBERS OF OUR FAMILY."

— HENRY FORD

In his landmark study of companies that made the leap from *Good to Great*, author Jim Collins found that great companies focused first on their people:

*"We found that they **first** got the right people on the bus, the wrong people off the bus, and the right people in the right seats—and **then** they figured out where to drive it. The old adage, 'People are your most important asset' turns out to be wrong. People are not your most important asset. The **right** people are."*

So what's the first step in getting the *right people on the bus*?

I'm a big fan of Nordstrom's, and my wife is a bigger fan. Recently, I had the opportunity to have lunch with a Nordstrom's executive and shared some of the great service moments his company had provided to the Anderson family. Then I asked the all-important question, "What is the key to Nordstrom's success? He answered as follows: "We hire great people and empower them to do whatever it takes to satisfy the customer." Then he continued, "We learned a long time ago that you can't send a duck to eagle school."

STEP 1: Get the Right People on the Bus

Get the Right People in the Right Seats STEP 2:

I said, "Excuse me?"

He elaborated: "You can't send a duck to eagle school. You can't teach someone to want to serve you, you can't teach a smile; you can't teach personality. However, you can hire people who have those qualities, and we can teach them our products and teach them our culture."

As leaders, how many of us are guilty of hiring ducks, thinking they could become eagles? I would be the first to raise my hand and admit it. What has happened, at least with me, is that I needed people quickly, and even knowing that they weren't exactly what I was looking for, I rationalized ("with a little work this duck could be an eagle") and hired them anyway. This can be, and usually is, one of the

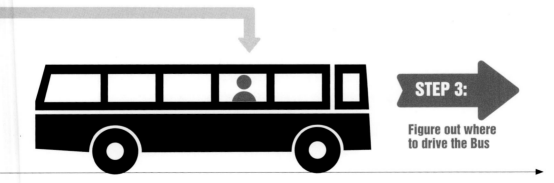

STEP 3:

Figure out where to drive the Bus

"I ALWAYS FELT THAT OUR PEOPLE CAME FIRST.

SOME OF THE BUSINESS SCHOOLS REGARDED THAT AS A CONUNDRUM. THEY WOULD SAY: WHICH COMES FIRST,

YOUR PEOPLE, YOUR CUSTOMERS, OR YOUR SHAREHOLDERS?

AND I WOULD SAY, IT'S NOT A CONUNDRUM. YOUR PEOPLE COME FIRST, AND IF YOU TREAT THEM RIGHT, THEY'LL TREAT THE CUSTOMERS RIGHT, AND THE CUSTOMERS WILL COME BACK, AND THAT'LL MAKE THE SHAREHOLDERS HAPPY."

— HERB KELLEHER,
FOUNDER, SOUTHWEST AIRLINES

most expensive mistakes any leader can make. You must constantly remind yourself that hiring the right person for your team is your most important job as a manager. With each hire, your credibility and your team's success are on the line.

Once they are Onboard, Treat Your People Right!

A 212° leader's responsibility doesn't end after hiring the right people; you have to treat them well to retain them. Here's a story from **Love 'Em or Lose 'Em** by Beverly Kaye and Sharon Jordan-Evans that drives the point home:

A successful accountant, tragically killed by a speeding bus, arrives at the Pearly Gates and is welcomed by St. Peter. St. Peter explains that she will need to spend one day in Heaven and one day in Hell before she decides where she would like to spend eternity.

With great trepidation she enters Hell and is amazed to find a beautiful golf course, friends, and colleagues who welcome her, terrific food, a great party, and even a nice-guy devil. At the end of her day, she regretfully leaves Hell in order to experience her day in Heaven. That experience is quite good also, with the clouds, angels, harps and singing that she expected.

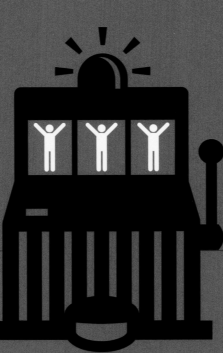

"I AM CONVINCED THAT NOTHING WE DO IS MORE IMPORTANT THAN HIRING AND DEVELOPING PEOPLE. AT THE END OF THE DAY

YOU BET ON PEOPLE, NOT ON STRATEGIES."

— LARRY BOSSIDY

"IF YOU PICK THE RIGHT PEOPLE AND GIVE THEM THE OPPORTUNITY TO SPREAD THEIR WINGS—AND PUT COMPENSATION AS A CARRIER BEHIND IT—YOU ALMOST DON'T HAVE TO MANAGE THEM."

— JACK WELCH

St. Peter pushes her to make the decision of a lifetime (and beyond). In which place would she spend eternity—Heaven or Hell? You guessed it—she chooses Hell. When she returns to Hell, she finds a desolate wasteland and her friends dressed in rags, picking up garbage. There are no parties—only misery and despair. She says to the Devil, "I don't understand. Yesterday I was here and there was a golf course and a country club, we ate lobster and danced and had a great time. Now I see a wasteland and all my friends look miserable." The Devil looks at her and smiles. "Yesterday we were recruiting you; today you're an employee."

When a study called ***Rewards at Work*** investigated how U.S. workers felt about the rewards they receive at work, the research showed that five reward categories were considered equally important by the workers:

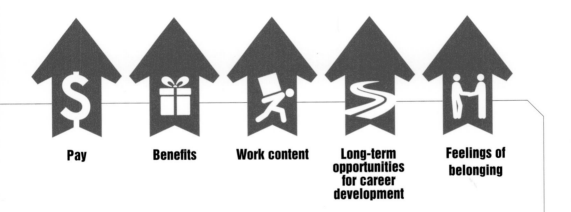

| Pay | Benefits | Work content | Long-term opportunities for career development | Feelings of belonging |

While there is no doubt that fair and competitive pay is one of the reasons that your employees show up to work every day, it's not the only reason. 212° leaders know that to retain great people you need to make your staff feel valued. Here are some tips from Robin Crow, author of ***Rock Solid Leadership:***

Use the five to one method. *For every one time you offer constructive criticism, make sure to acknowledge them for five things they've done right.*

→ **Praise them on the spot.** *The sooner you praise them after the event, the more meaningful it is to them. So praise while the moment is hot.*

→ **Acknowledge them publicly for others to see.** *There's nothing more important to people than significance and recognition.*

→ **Find creative ways to reward good behavior.** *Unexpected rewards like giving extra time off or spontaneously taking that person to lunch will reap great dividends.*

A paycheck is what an employee works for. Recognition and praise is what they live for! One of the greatest challenges for managers is finding creative ways to fill that need. Many times, this one thing can be the difference between a good and a great leader.

"ALWAYS TREAT YOUR EMPLOYEES EXACTLY AS YOU WANT THEM TO TREAT YOUR BEST CUSTOMERS."
— STEPHEN COVEY

"**PEOPLE**
ARE DEFINITELY A COMPANY'S
GREATEST ASSET.
IT DOESN'T MAKE ANY DIFFERENCE
WHETHER THE PRODUCT IS CARS
OR COSMETICS.
**A COMPANY IS ONLY
AS GOOD AS THE
PEOPLE IT KEEPS.**"

— MARY KAY ASH

CHAPTER 3

SIMPLIFY YOUR VISION FOR SUCCESS

→ *"A leader's job is to look into the future and see the organization not as it is, but as it should be."*

— *Jack Welch*

Lewis Carroll said, "If you don't know where you are going, any road will get you there."

If your team doesn't know where they are going, how will they know that they've arrived?

Sharing your vision... in a way that energizes your team... is one of the most important steps you'll take as a 212° leader.

In his book, **Leading with Passion**, John J. Murphy gives this example of how important vision can be to business success:

Imagine you are sitting blindfolded with a tinker toy model on a table in front of you, just out of reach. Your task is to reproduce the model in less than two minutes. You cannot touch the model, but you do have a supervisor who can provide you with limited feedback and you have all the supplies you need. Unfortunately, your supervisor has been instructed to provide you with negative feedback only!

Can you imagine how you might feel? You do not know exactly what to make and every time you grab the wrong part you are told

"no" or "wrong." If you happen to grab the right part, you hear nothing at all. Not very inspiring, is it? Yet this simple demonstration represents the "disconnect" people all over the world frequently feel when the vision is not clear and they are not supported with positive direction and feedback.

Now let's try another round of the exercise. This time, imagine you are still blindfolded with two minutes to reproduce the model, but your supervisor can now provide you with positive feedback. In other words, if you grab a part you need, your supervisor will say "yes" or "right." Participants in this round generally report feeling much better about the task and the work environment, but there is still not much authentic

"GOOD BUSINESS LEADERS CREATE A VISION, ARTICULATE THE VISION, PASSIONATELY OWN THE VISION, AND RELENTLESSLY DRIVE IT TO COMPLETION."

— JACK WELCH

spirit in the work. The clock winds down and no one gets it quite right. Progress has been made and confidence is higher, but performance is still weak. Some participants even ask for "more time," convinced they can get it right. More time and resources are a common response when people and organizations fall behind. We need more people! We need more capital! We need more capacity! We need more inventory! We need more time! The visionary leader challenges this common paradigm of scarcity by asking if there is anything obstructing our view. Is there anything constraining us? What might we do to facilitate better flow and understanding?

Cultivating a passionate and inspiring work environment requires clear and compelling vision that is shared by the team. It is simply not enough for one person to see the "desired state" and everyone else to guess at it.

Your vision for your organization's success is just your starting point. Everyone must be "marching to the same drummer" … and to do that you need to simplify your message. Need some examples?

After schooling in the States, Roberto Goizueta returned to Cuba in 1953 to work in his family's sugar business; but he was soon scanning want ads. He answered an anonymous ad for work at a Cola-Cola® bottling plant in Cuba. There he would begin a famous career marked by his unique ability to inspire people.

In 1979, Goizueta was named the president of The Cola-Cola Company, and in 1981, the company's chairman. Over a 16-year span, Goizueta created more wealth for shareholders than any CEO in the company's history and made Coca-Cola® the most prominent trademark in the world.

Though English was his third language, his success is primarily attributed to his ability to encapsulate complex ideas and present them in concise, compelling fashion. Roberto was best known for his oft-repeated description of Coke's infinite growth potential:

Each of the six billion people on this planet drinks, on average, sixty-four ounces of fluids daily, of which only two ounces are Coca-Cola®.

Coke's employees were blown away by the originality and audacity of the idea when Goizueta first spoke it. Eventually, closing the "sixty-two ounce gap" became a centerpiece of inspiration and motivation within the company.

When it comes to articulating your company's vision … the simpler the better. Joe Calhoon and Bruce Jeffrey are consultants who specialize in helping companies create a simple one-page, strategic plan. I love the idea because there is something magic about one page. Here are the six key elements of the plan:

THE ONE-PAGE STRATEGIC PLAN

1	**VISION**	A clear picture of your destination
2	**MISSION**	The driving purpose of your business
3	**VALUES**	The guide you use for decision making and how you treat each other
4	**OBJECTIVES**	The numbers you track
5	**STRATEGIES**	The paths you've decided to take
6	**PRIORITIES**	The work that needs to get done and who needs to do it.

"A LEADER HAS THE
VISION AND CONVICTION
THAT A DREAM CAN BE ACHIEVED.
HE INSPIRES THE
POWER AND ENERGY
TO GET IT DONE."

— RALPH NADER

According to Calhoon and Jeffrey, they've never seen a plan that was too short, but they have seen hundreds that make an acceptable cure for insomnia. ***They also said that once the management team understands the process, they have never encountered a company that couldn't fit their plan on one page.***

Does it take a little more time to "drill down?" Sure it does, but it's well worth it because it forces you to cut out a lot of verbiage and make decisions on what's most important.

Your company's mission is a statement about what you stand for and where you are going—it is your ship's rudder.

> **"VISION WITHOUT ACTION IS A DREAM. ACTION WITHOUT VISION IS SIMPLY PASSING THE TIME. ACTION WITH VISION IS MAKING A POSITIVE DIFFERENCE."**
> — JOEL BARKER

"THE VERY ESSENCE OF LEADERSHIP IS **YOU HAVE A VISION.** IT'S GOT TO BE A VISION YOU ARTICULATE CLEARLY AND FORCEFULLY ON EVERY OCCASION. **YOU CAN'T BLOW AN UNCERTAIN TRUMPET.**"

— THEODORE HESBURGH

"A VISION IS NOT JUST A PICTURE OF WHAT COULD BE; IT IS AN APPEAL TO OUR BETTER SELVES, A CALL TO BECOME SOMETHING MORE."

— ROSABETH MOSS KANTER

CHAPTER 4

REMEMBER
OLD
WARWICK

 "Teamwork is the fuel that allows common people to attain uncommon results."
— *Andrew Carnegie*

With your vision firmly in place, it's time to create an atmosphere where your entire team is pulling in the same direction. A friend sent me the story of "Old Warwick." It brought a smile to my face, and I think it shares a wonderful lesson for every leader to learn:

A man was lost while driving through the country. As he tried to reach for the map, he accidentally drove off the road into a ditch. Though he wasn't injured, his car was stuck deep in the mud. So the man walked to a nearby farm to ask for help. **"Warwick can get you out of that ditch,"** *said the farmer, pointing to an old mule standing in a field. The man looked at the decrepit old mule and looked at the farmer who just stood there repeating,* **"Yep, old Warwick can do the job."** *The man figured he had nothing to lose. The two men and the mule made their way back to the ditch. The farmer hitched one mule to the car. With a snap of the reins he shouted,*

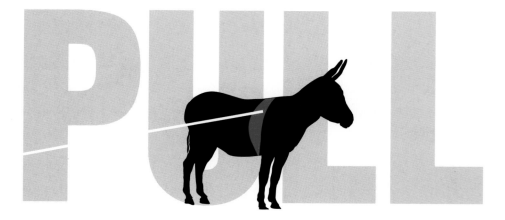

"Pull, Fred! Pull, Jack! Pull, Ted Pull,
Pull Warwick!"

And the mule pulled that car right out of the ditch.

The man was amazed. He thanked the farmer, patted the mule, and asked, "Why did you call out all of those names before you called Warwick?"

The farmer grinned and said, **"Old Warwick is just about blind. As long as he believes he's part of a team, he doesn't mind pulling."**

Adapted from *Some Folks Feel the Rain: Others Just Get Wet*, by James W. Moore.

"COOPERATION
IS THE THOROUGH CONVICTION THAT
NOBODY CAN GET THERE UNLESS
EVERYBODY GETS THERE."
— VIRGINIA BURDEN

"PEOPLE ACTING TOGETHER

AS A GROUP CAN ACCOMPLISH THINGS WHICH

NO INDIVIDUAL

ACTING ALONE COULD

EVER HOPE TO BRING ABOUT."

— FRANKLIN DELANO ROOSEVELT

Over the past 25 years, there has been an upward trend in how great companies view the value of teamwork. Here's how John C. Maxwell describes it:

In the 1980s, the word was management. *The idea was that a manager was needed to create consistency. (The goal was to keep standards from slipping.)*

In the 1990s, the key concept was leadership by an individual. *Organizations saw that leaders were needed because everything was changing so quickly.*

In the 2000s, the idea is team leadership. *Because leading an organization has become so complex and multifaceted, the only way to make progress is to develop a team of leaders.*

UPWARD TREND OF THE VALUE OF TEAMWORK.

1990s

1980s

INDIVIDUAL LEADERSHIP

MANAGEMENT

2000s

TEAM LEADERSHIP

"THE STRENGTH OF THE TEAM IS EACH INDIVIDUAL MEMBER... THE STRENGTH OF EACH MEMBER IS THE TEAM."

— PHIL JACKSON

48

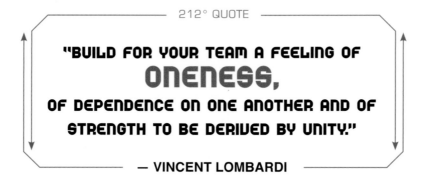

212° QUOTE

"BUILD FOR YOUR TEAM A FEELING OF
ONENESS,
OF DEPENDENCE ON ONE ANOTHER AND OF
STRENGTH TO BE DERIVED BY UNITY."

— VINCENT LOMBARDI

212° leaders understand the dynamic energy of teamwork … of fostering an environment where synergies are formed, with a shared commitment to achieving the organization's goals.

Nowhere is that philosophy displayed more than in the ultimate team—the world's best flight performance team—the Blue Angels. With life or death consequences for their actions, these extraordinary service men of the U.S. Navy truly know the meaning of teamwork.

In their book *The Power of Teamwork*, which was inspired by the Blue Angels, authors Scott Beare and Michael McMillan share one of the key elements of teamwork—fostering positive attitudes

Attitudes are highly contagious within a team structure. Because they can serve as self-fulfilling prophecies, they have the power to destroy a team or accelerate it to great heights. That's why there's no place for a bad attitude. **Each team member is responsible to one another for staying upbeat and positive.** *When everyone embraces this thinking, the entire team radiates with positive energy and appears unstoppable. A "can't do" attitude does just the opposite. It drains energy and poisons the team. Since attitudes can spread like a forest fire out of control, it's important to extinguish the bad ones and replace them with optimistic can-do attitudes—and do so*

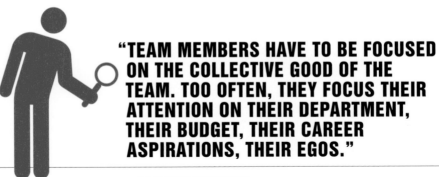

"TEAM MEMBERS HAVE TO BE FOCUSED ON THE COLLECTIVE GOOD OF THE TEAM. TOO OFTEN, THEY FOCUS THEIR ATTENTION ON THEIR DEPARTMENT, THEIR BUDGET, THEIR CAREER ASPIRATIONS, THEIR EGOS."

— PATRICK LENCIONI

*without delay. In addition to setting the standard, **leaders must know the pulse of the team and ensure positive attitudes prevail from top to bottom.** When people focus on what can be done rather than what can't, they align to create a positive team environment fueled by sustainable momentum.*

We can't choose many of the challenges we will face in this life, but we can choose how we will address them. *Teams that foster creative and optimistic thinking have the proper foundation in place for unlimited success.*

If you want to be a 212° leader, do you have a can-do attitude? Is the pulse of your team negative or positive? Does the environment foster optimistic thinking? How do you add to the team's outlook?

"A GROUP BECOMES A TEAM WHEN EACH MEMBER IS SURE ENOUGH OF **HIMSELF** AND HIS CONTRIBUTION TO PRAISE THE SKILLS OF THE OTHERS."

— NORMAN S. HIDLE

CHAPTER 5

COMMUNICATE
COMMUNICATE
COMMUNICATE

→ *"The single biggest problem in communication is the illusion that it has taken place."*
— *George Bernard Shaw*

Information is power. 212° leaders know that if they want their employees to have the power to achieve the company's vision, they need to have the information to do so.

In **The Breakthrough Company**, Keith McFarland describes the importance of effective communication:

During difficult times, many leaders tend to hunker down, cutting off communications with the rest of the folks in the company. And they usually mean well: They are afraid that if they share any shred of bad news it will spook the troops. Ironically, by dramatically decreasing the amount of information they share, some leaders virtually guarantee the very problems they're trying to avoid. Everyone lives each day on the edge, and rumors fly around the water cooler and coffee room. When you cut off the flow of information to the troops in difficult times, you leave them to develop their own negative fantasies about what's happening, and they often dream up doomsday scenarios that are far worse than the reality. Company leaders who communicate often and honestly, on the other hand, convey both the gravity of the situation along with the confidence that the firm is working toward a solution—and could sure use the rest of the company's support to get there.

So, just what is a 212° leader supposed to share? In her book, ***The Truth about Being a Leader***, Dr. Karen Otazo says there are three keys to effective communication:

1 WHAT'S HAPPENING...

Share as much as you can about the company's goals and current projects, especially any good news ... but, also be proactive if things aren't going as planned.

WHAT'S COMING UP...

2

This is a bit like "coming attractions." Your team is always interested in what's new.

3

HOW THEY'RE DOING...

This one is critical. Look for opportunities, private and public, to say good things, or talk about how they could do better. Most people want to know how they're doing, but are afraid to ask. It is very important to visit, and connect with team members personally.

The 212° leader truly understands that providing effective feedback can be the key to outstanding performance. Here's how Ken Blanchard describes it in his book, ***The Heart of a Leader:***

There are three responses people can receive from leadership concerning their performance—positive, negative, or no response at all. Only one response of the three tends to increase good performance— the positive one. And yet, the major leadership style used today is "leave alone—zap!"

POSSIBLE RESPONSES RECEIVED FROM LEADERSHIP

"Feedback is the breakfast of champions."
— **KEN BLANCHARD**

A person who does something correctly and receives a positive response will most likely continue that desired behavior in the future. By the same token, a person who receives a negative response for doing something wrong will most likely not repeat the behavior. But what if someone does something correctly and receives no response at all? The behavior may continue for awhile, but eventually it will decline. Why? Because no one seems to care.

"COMMUNICATION WORKS
FOR THOSE WHO WORK AT IT."
— **JOHN POWELL**

58

"THE DIFFERENCE BETWEEN THE ALMOST RIGHT WORD AND THE RIGHT WORD IS REALLY A LARGE MATTER— IT'S THE DIFFERENCE BETWEEN THE LIGHTNING AND THE LIGHTNING BUG."

— MARK TWAIN

Many leaders notice their people doing things right and think well of them. Unfortunately, they do not always put those positive thoughts into words. As a result, this good performance gets no response. If you want to get and maintain good performance, you must let your people know you notice and care about the things they do right. Share your good thoughts.

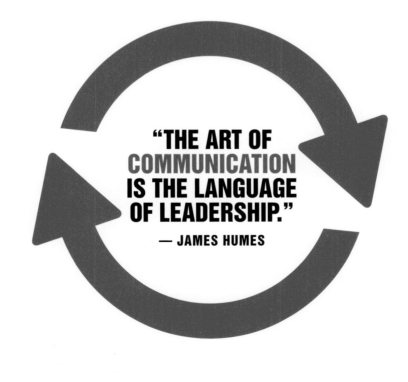

"THE ART OF COMMUNICATION IS THE LANGUAGE OF LEADERSHIP."
— JAMES HUMES

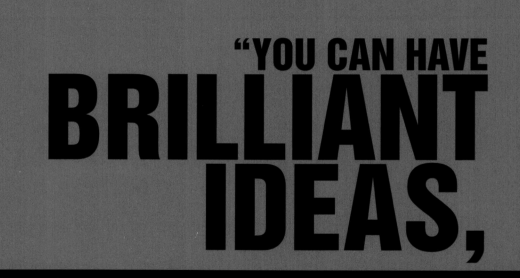

"YOU CAN HAVE
BRILLIANT
IDEAS,

BUT IF YOU CAN'T GET THEM ACROSS, YOUR IDEAS WON'T GET YOU ANYWHERE."

— LEE IACOCCA

CHAPTER 6

SET THE
STAGE FOR
INNOVATION

→ *"You cannot discover new oceans
unless you have the courage to lose
sight of the shore."*
— *Lord Chesterfield*

Linus Pauling said, "The way to get a good idea is to get lots of ideas." Not rocket science, but it works!

The only way to keep a change culture alive, long-term, is to set the stage for innovation. Kevin Kelly, in his book, **New Rules for the New Economy** said, "Wealth today flows directly from innovation, not optimization. It is not gained by perfecting the known, but by imperfectly seizing the unknown."

Tomorrow comes at us with lightning speed, and your competitive advantage is a fleeting thing. As leaders, we must create an environment that puts innovation front and center. Your people must know it is the key to your company's survival. You must create a climate that rewards risk and creative effort. Your people must not fear mistakes, but understand that honest mistakes can be life's main source for learning. So teach them to fail quickly, and often, to enable them to reach the next plateau.

Far too many leaders consider innovation the business equivalent of football's "Hail Mary" pass or the buzzer-beating three-pointer in basketball. On rare occasions it might work, but "rare occasions," and "might work" are not the foundation of effective innovation programs. Innovation requires a system, a culture, leadership, and an allocation of resources. Then, it becomes a matter of discipline, commitment and determination.

Tom Peters gets it. He said… "I've spent a good part of my life studying economic successes and failures. Above all, I've learned that everything takes a back seat to innovation."

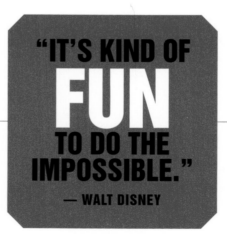

"IT'S KIND OF FUN TO DO THE IMPOSSIBLE."
— WALT DISNEY

"LIFE IS CHANGE. GROWTH IS OPTIONAL. CHOOSE WISELY."

— KAREN KAISER CLARK

Before You Can Innovate You Have to Embrace Change ...

Consider this. A little over a hundred years ago ...

	There were only 8,000 cars in the United States and 144 miles of paved road.
	The average U.S. worker made between $200 and $400 a year.
	Only eight percent of homes had a telephone.
	Alabama, Mississippi, Iowa and Tennessee were all more populated than California.
	Only six percent of Americans had graduated from high school.

We must never forget…

Change is inevitable, but growth is optional.

Of all U.S. companies, 3M is probably the most famous in creating a culture of innovation, or "disciplined creativity," as some call it. This didn't happen by accident. In 1929, founder William McKnight turned innovation into a systematic, reputable process. He rewarded the lone spirits within the company who were "given permission" to fight for their new ideas. The innovative creative culture has fueled many success stories along the way, including the development of Post-it Notes®. Although Post-its failed their initial market test, the 3M scientist who invented the product hooked a core group of users by distributing free samples to the staff at headquarters in Minneapolis. He was allowed to fight for his product's success, and the rest, as they say, is history.

"IT IS NOT NECESSARY TO CHANGE. SURVIVAL IS NOT MANDATORY."
— W. EDWARDS DEMING

"INNOVATION DISTINGUISHES BETWEEN A LEADER AND A FOLLOWER."

— STEVE JOBS

As a 212° leader, how can you put your company in a position to exploit change? It's not easy.

According to Peter Drucker, most companies find it less difficult to come up with new ideas than to let go of old ones. I certainly agree with him that most leaders are too busy solving today's problems to focus on tomorrow's opportunities. It's human nature. To put innovation on the "front burner," Drucker recommends that your monthly operating report have two pages: one listing the problems and one targeting "possible opportunities."

This, he says, will force each leader to keep innovation and continuous improvement front and center. In fact, Drucker recommends that every three years each product, process and distribution channel should be put on trial for its life.

One thing is certain: innovation starts with creative people who are allowed to take risks and be rewarded for their efforts.

CHAPTER 7

COMMIT TO
EXCELLENCE

 *"Excellence is not a skill.
It is an attitude."*

—Ralph Marsten

Quality is the Mother ... And We Don't Mess with Mom

We embraced this "quality motto" early on at Successories and I was greatly influenced by my creative partner and friend, Michael McKee. Our paper stock, our color separations, our frames, and even our shipping cartons were of the highest quality. It was one of our core values.

I recall an incident in 1988 when we were at about $5 million in sales. Cash was tight and we were watching every penny. Mike brought a copy of a new print into my office. It had just come off the press. As we were congratulating one another, my assistant walked in and pointed to an apostrophe in the quote at the bottom of the print. It should have come before the "S" instead of behind the "S." Michael and I sat there stunned, because to reprint it would have cost approximately $5,000, which unfortunately we didn't have at the time. Although we both knew that 999 people out of 1,000 wouldn't notice the misplaced apostrophe, our commitment to quality gave us only one choice… destroy the prints and start over. It was a gut-wrenching decision, given our financial situation, but the right one. It left no doubt with our team that we were willing to walk the talk when it came to quality.

In his book, **Pulling Together**, John J. Murphy outlines the importance for leaders to commit to excellence:

One of the most vital bonds holding high performance teams together is a common commitment to excellence—a united quest for on-going improvement. Every player recognizes the need for raising the standards and setting new records. The marketplace does not relax. The competition is not going to let up. Customer expectations will not diminish. The glory days of the past will not protect us in the future. Each day brings with it a new challenge, an opportunity to excel beyond yesterday.

"EXCELLENCE IS TO DO A COMMON THING IN AN UNCOMMON WAY."

— BOOKER T. WASHINGTON

Remember that it is this perception that creates a vital link between team members, especially during times of adversity and loss. Each player must recognize a genuine commitment from one another, making mistakes more tolerable and burdens easier to carry. Committing to excellence means sharing the risk required in generating maximum returns and pursuing victory together. Effective team players know that achieving peak performance requires positive attitudes and inspiring beliefs on everyone's part. Sustaining peak performance requires humility, dignity and grace.

"DESIRE IS THE KEY
TO MOTIVATION, BUT IT'S DETERMINATION AND COMMITMENT TO AN UNRELENTING PURSUIT OF YOUR GOAL—A COMMITMENT TO EXCELLENCE—THAT WILL ENABLE YOU TO ATTAIN THE SUCCESS YOU SEEK."

— MARIO ANDRETTI

"EXCELLENCE IS IN THE DETAILS. GIVE ATTENTION TO THE DETAILS AND EXCELLENCE WILL COME."
— PERRY PAXTON

Watch a competitive athlete make an honest error in a game and observe how quickly his teammates offer encouragement and support. What's this? Comfort for a mistake? A pat on the back for a mishap? How can this be? People are paid to do things right, not screw them up! Now examine your own organization. How are errors in your work environment perceived? How are mistakes handled? Are people given support for taking calculated risks and falling short? Or punished? What is the price for learning and stretching in your world?

"THE SECRET OF JOY IN WORK
IS CONTAINED IN ONE WORD—
EXCELLENCE.
TO KNOW HOW TO DO
SOMETHING WELL
IS TO ENJOY IT."
— PEARL BUCK

High performance teams view honest mistakes as part of the learning process. Given everyone on the team is committed to excellence, they review what went wrong, why it went wrong, and then focus on what needs to change. They move forward, recognizing that making no mistakes often implies they are not taking enough risks, not stretching far enough, not learning fast enough. Playing it safe does not elevate people to peak performance. We have to dare to get a hit, recognizing that "striking out" is part of the same process. Give it some thought.

When you look in the mirror, do you see a person committed to excellence, a tenacious team member striving for total quality?

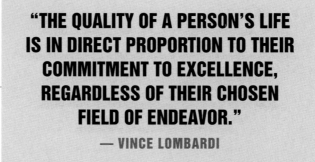

"THE QUALITY OF A PERSON'S LIFE IS IN DIRECT PROPORTION TO THEIR COMMITMENT TO EXCELLENCE, REGARDLESS OF THEIR CHOSEN FIELD OF ENDEAVOR."
— VINCE LOMBARDI

"IF YOU ARE GOING TO ACHIEVE EXCELLENCE IN BIG THINGS, YOU DEVELOP THE HABIT IN LITTLE MATTERS. EXCELLENCE IS NOT AN EXCEPTION, IT IS A PREVAILING ATTITUDE."

— COLIN POWELL

CHAPTER 8

TAKE
FULL
RESPONSIBILITY

→ *"It is the responsibility of leadership to provide opportunity, and the responsibility of individuals to contribute."*
— *William Pollard*

Something magic happens when we accept personal responsibility for our behavior and our results. But it's not easy, because it's human nature to "pass the buck."

I know there have been times in my life when my business was struggling where I found myself blaming others, blaming the economy, blaming this, blaming that! But as I've gotten older (and a little wiser) when things go wrong in my business, or my life, I can always find the culprit … in the mirror. In every instance, it always comes back to choices I've made in my life that put me exactly where I am today. I have to say, that this one "tweak" in my attitude may sound like a little thing, but it has made a big difference in my life.

"YOU MUST TAKE PERSONAL RESPONSIBILITY. YOU CANNOT CHANGE THE CIRCUMSTANCES, THE SEASONS, OR THE WIND,
BUT YOU CAN CHANGE YOURSELF.
THAT IS SOMETHING YOU HAVE CHARGE OF."
— JIM ROHN

As a 212° leader, one of the most important things you can do is to get your people to understand how their taking personal responsibility, their recognizing problems as opportunities, will not only help the company, but will help them as individuals. In other words, sell the idea of… what's in it for them.

Authors B.J.Gallagher and Steve Ventura wrote a great little book about achieving success through personal accountability titled: *Who are "They" Anyway?* I like their list showing how each individual in the company can benefit by adopting a "personal accountability attitude:"

PERSONAL ACCOUNTABILITY
ATTITUDE

→ **YOU** have more control over your destiny

→ **YOU** become an active contributor rather than a passive observer

→ **OTHERS** look to you for leadership

→ **YOU** gain the reputation as a problem solver

→ **YOU** enhance your career opportunities

→ **YOU** enjoy the satisfaction that comes from getting things done ... the power of positive doing

→ **YOU** experience less anger, frustration and helplessness—all leading to better physical health

→ **YOU** realize a positive spillover effect into your personal life at home

According to Gallagher and Ventura, the most important words of personal responsibility are as follows:

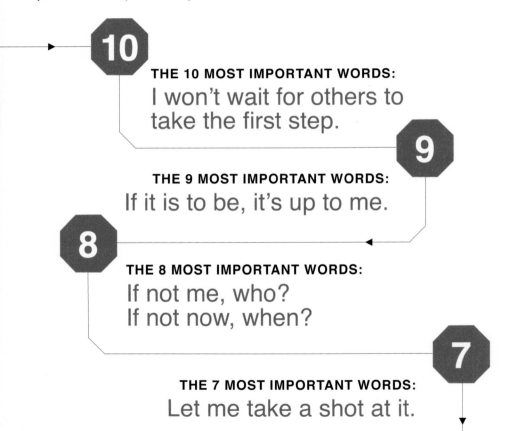

THE 10 MOST IMPORTANT WORDS:
I won't wait for others to take the first step.

THE 9 MOST IMPORTANT WORDS:
If it is to be, it's up to me.

THE 8 MOST IMPORTANT WORDS:
If not me, who?
If not now, when?

THE 7 MOST IMPORTANT WORDS:
Let me take a shot at it.

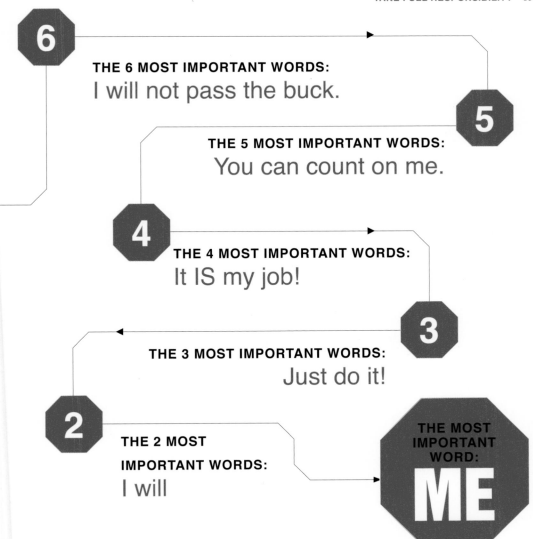

THE 6 MOST IMPORTANT WORDS:
I will not pass the buck.

THE 5 MOST IMPORTANT WORDS:
You can count on me.

THE 4 MOST IMPORTANT WORDS:
It IS my job!

THE 3 MOST IMPORTANT WORDS:
Just do it!

THE 2 MOST IMPORTANT WORDS:
I will

THE MOST IMPORTANT WORD:
ME

"YOU CAN DELEGATE AUTHORITY, BUT NOT RESPONSIBILITY."

— STEPHEN W. COMISKEY

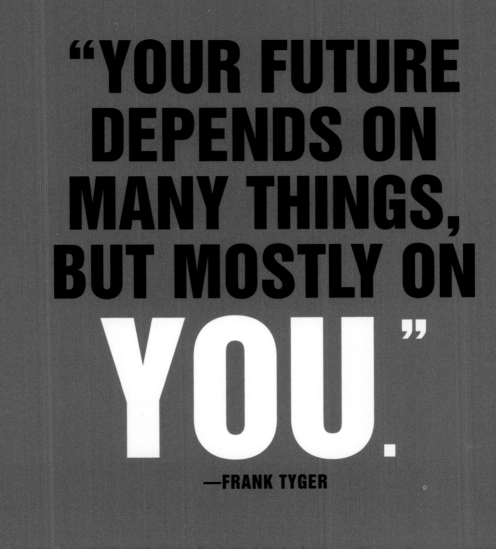

"YOUR FUTURE DEPENDS ON MANY THINGS, BUT MOSTLY ON YOU."

—FRANK TYGER

CHAPTER 9

MEASURE
RESULTS

→ *"What gets measured, gets improved."*
— *Peter Drucker*

Most employees want to grow, they want to do better, they want to take pride in their work, but they need targets to shoot for. Unless they have clearly defined goals, the "path of least resistance" will almost always raise its ugly head.

In the words of Peter Drucker, ***"What we measure gets improved."***
John C. Maxwell has an example from the life of Charles Schwab, who once ran U.S. Steel, which drives the point home:

It was near the end of the day; in a few minutes the night force would come on duty. I turned to a workman who was standing beside one of the red-mouthed furnaces and asked him for a piece of chalk.

"How many heats has your shift made today?" I queried.

"Six," he replied.

I chalked a big "6" on the floor, and then passed along without another word. When the night shift came in, they saw the "6" and asked about it.

6 7 10

"The big boss was in here today," said the day men. "He asked us how many heats we had made, and we told him six. He chalked it down."

The next morning I passed through the same mill. I saw that the "6" had been rubbed out and a big "7" written instead. The night shift had announced itself. That night I went back. The "7" had been erased and a "10" swaggered in its place. The day force recognized no superiors. Thus a fine competition was started, and it went on until this mill, formerly the poorest producer, was turning out more than the other mill in the plant.

> **"YOUR SUCCESS IN LIFE ISN'T BASED ON YOUR ABILITY TO SIMPLY CHANGE. IT IS BASED ON YOUR ABILITY TO CHANGE FASTER THAN YOUR COMPETITION, CUSTOMERS AND BUSINESS."**
>
> **— MARK SANBORN**

"WHAT DO YOU WANT TO ACHIEVE OR AVOID?

THE ANSWERS TO THIS QUESTION ARE **OBJECTIVES.**

HOW WILL YOU GO ABOUT ACHIEVING YOUR DESIRED RESULTS?

THE ANSWER TO THIS YOU CAN CALL **STRATEGY.**"

— WILLIAM E ROTHSCHILD

As a 212° leader, you have to ask yourself:

What activities can I measure to track our progress?

First, of course, you must determine where you are now with each activity you wish to improve. Secondly, you need to set realistic targets for improvement. Thirdly, and most importantly, you must track, monitor, and review results on a daily, weekly and monthly basis. Now this may sound boring, but it is critical to break old habits and to inspire new thinking.

DETERMINE WHERE YOU ARE NOW

SET REALISTIC TARGETS FOR IMPROVEMENT

YOU MUST TRACK, MONITOR, AND REVIEW RESULTS

> **"THE RESULTS YOU ACHIEVE WILL BE IN DIRECT PROPORTION TO THE EFFORT YOU APPLY."**
>
> **— DENIS WAITLEY**

Here are just a few examples of what could be measured to track your progress:

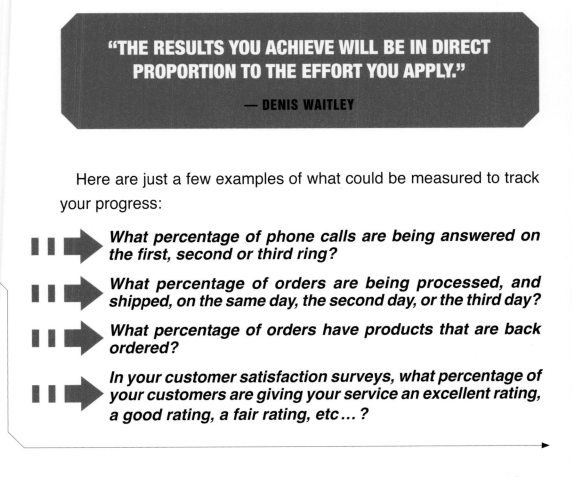

What percentage of phone calls are being answered on the first, second or third ring?

What percentage of orders are being processed, and shipped, on the same day, the second day, or the third day?

What percentage of orders have products that are back ordered?

In your customer satisfaction surveys, what percentage of your customers are giving your service an excellent rating, a good rating, a fair rating, etc ... ?

Are we making progress toward our goal?

"THE GREATER DANGER FOR MOST OF US LIES NOT IN SETTING OUR **AIM TOO HIGH** AND FALLING SHORT; BUT IN SETTING OUR **AIM TOO LOW,** AND ACHIEVING OUR MARK."

— MICHELANGELO

CHAPTER 10

EXAMPLE
IS MOST
IMPORTANT

> "A leader leads by example,
> whether he intends to or not."
> — John Quincy Adams

What example did you set today? When you lead by example, you engage your people to follow your vision … not by words, but by action. While you are measuring your employees' performance, they are measuring how well you follow through on both your words and your deeds.

Think leading by example is only for top management? Think again. Whatever your position in your organization, the way you do your job … *and the attitude with which you do it* … determines the impact that you have.

"LEADERSHIP IS PRACTICED NOT SO MUCH IN WORDS AS IN ATTITUDE AND IN ACTIONS."

— HAROLD S. GENEEN

I recently read a story by Mark Brown in the ***Chicago Sun-Times*** that really drives this point home. Mark wrote about a Chicago-area mailman, Mike Martinez, who passed away at the age of 50, but left a lasting impression by the example he set:

"Mike was a heckuva nice guy who knew everyone on his route by name and always greeted them with a smile, a wave and some friendly chitchat.

"He was the kind of mailman who would warn them if they'd forgotten to move their cars on street-sweeping day, search the post office on his weekend day off for their missing package or stop by their homes after work for a beer or a barbecue."

"GOOD LEADERS MUST BECOME WHAT THEY WANT **THEIR FOLLOWERS TO BECOME.**"

— NIDO R. QUBEIN

The article goes on to describe other people that Mike touched as he delivered the mail, including Tom Lutz, who had suffered a stroke. Mike would call Tom and ask him to help deliver the mail to his neighbors as part of his rehab.

"He would encourage me to try a little harder each day, as my bad leg would get better little by little," said Tom.

"Martinez was such an unforgettable character, in fact, that some of those customers built a memorial garden in his honor.

"I've never seen anything quite like 'Mike's Corner,' certainly not for a mailman. The garden consists of an exquisitely landscaped corner parkway plot with a small stone monument topped by an old-fashioned flag mailbox and a plaque designed to look like a letter. The letter to Mike T. Martinez Jr. carries a return address of 'Rest in Peace 1959-2010'.

> **"TRUST IS NOT A MATTER OF TECHNIQUE, BUT OF CHARACTER. WE ARE TRUSTED BECAUSE OF OUR WAY OF BEING, NOT BECAUSE OF OUR POLISHED EXTERIORS OR OUR EXPERTLY CRAFTED COMMUNICATIONS."**
> — MARSHA SINETAR

"You don't need to have a big-shot job to leave your mark in this world. All it takes is a warm smile, an upbeat attitude and a kind heart."

There's no doubt about it. Mike left some big shoes to fill along his route … but that challenge to achieve the same connection with those he served is part of his legacy.

"'It really makes you step up your game,' said mail carrier Tamme Price as she worked his old route."

That's the power of a living example. It can make those around you "step up their game," … sometimes long after you are gone.

Jeff Gitomer, author of the **Little Book of Leadership** said it best, "Your people are a direct reflection of you. They watch you. They follow you. They measure you. They listen to you. If you want them to be dedicated to you, you have to be dedicated to them."

Through your words, actions and deeds, you set the foundation for building an environment of trust and respect.

"YOU MUST BE CAREFUL HOW YOU WALK, THOSE FOLLOWING YOU WHO WILL

Trust is the key to both managing people and building a high performance company. It is the foundation on which relationships are built. According to Tom Peters, "Technique and technology are important. *But adding trust is the issue of the decade."* Peters suggests that managers must take a "high-tech and high-trust" approach, putting the issue of trust at the top of the agenda and

AND WHERE YOU GO, FOR THERE ARE SET THEIR FEET WHERE YOURS ARE SET."

— ROBERT E. LEE

treating it like a "hard issue, not a soft issue." If employees feel you don't trust them to do their jobs correctly and well, they'll be reluctant to do much without your approval. On the other hand, when they feel trusted that you believe they'll do the right things well, they'll naturally want to do things to the best of their ability and be deserving of your trust.

In ***On Becoming a Leader***, Warren Bennis outlines the four ingredients for leaders to generate and sustain trust:

 Constancy.

Whatever surprises leaders themselves may face, they don't create any for the group. Leaders stay the course.

 Congruity.

Leaders walk their talk. In true leaders, there is no gap between the theories they espouse and the life they practice.

 Reliability.

Leaders are there when it counts; they are ready to support their co-workers in the moments that matter.

 Integrity.

Leaders honor their commitments and promises.

"EXAMPLE IS NOT THE MAIN THING IN INFLUENCING OTHERS.

> **"TRUST MEN AND THEY WILL BE TRUE TO YOU;
> TREAT THEM GREATLY, AND THEY WILL
> SHOW THEMSELVES GREAT."**
> — RALPH WALDO EMERSON

While corporate scandals, terrorist threats, office politics, and broken relationships have created low trust on almost every front, I contend that the ability to establish, grow, extend, and restore trust is not only vital to our personal and interpersonal well-being, it is the key leadership competency of the new global economy.

I am also convinced in every situation, ***nothing is as fast as the speed of trust.***

IT IS THE ONLY THING." — ALBERT SCHWEITZER

CONCLUSION

Some people think great leaders are born. But I don't. I think leadership skills can be honed.

You don't have to be a good leader to get people to follow you on an unchanging course. You can be an average leader and some will still follow you through minor bends in the road. But to get people to follow you through unpredictable twists and turns, you must not only sell your vision, you must show you care. You must make the leap from good to great …

You must be a 212° leader.
Are you ready for the challenge?

Mac Anderson is the founder of Simple Truths and Successories, Inc., the leader in designing and marketing products for motivation and recognition. These companies, however, are not the first success stories for Mac. He was also the founder and CEO of McCord Travel, the largest travel company in the Midwest, and part owner/VP of sales and marketing for Orval Kent Food Company, the country's largest manufacturer of prepared salads.

His accomplishments in these unrelated industries provide some insight into his passion and leadership skills. He also brings the same passion to his speaking when he speaks to many corporate audiences on a variety of topics, including leadership, motivation, and team building.

Mac has authored or co-authored 18 books that have sold over four million copies. His titles include:

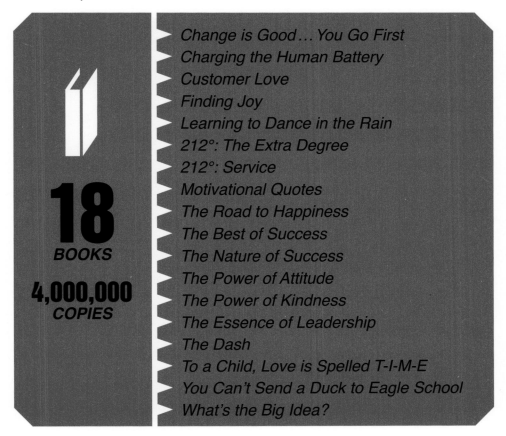

18 BOOKS

4,000,000 COPIES

- *Change is Good… You Go First*
- *Charging the Human Battery*
- *Customer Love*
- *Finding Joy*
- *Learning to Dance in the Rain*
- *212°: The Extra Degree*
- *212°: Service*
- *Motivational Quotes*
- *The Road to Happiness*
- *The Best of Success*
- *The Nature of Success*
- *The Power of Attitude*
- *The Power of Kindness*
- *The Essence of Leadership*
- *The Dash*
- *To a Child, Love is Spelled T-I-M-E*
- *You Can't Send a Duck to Eagle School*
- *What's the Big Idea?*

For more information about Mac, visit www.simpletruths.com

WHAT OTHERS ARE SAYING...

WE PURCHASED A SIMPLE TRUTHS GIFT BOOK FROM OUR CONFERENCE IN LISBON, SPAIN. WE ALSO PERSONALIZED IT WITH A NOTE ON THE FIRST PAGE ABOUT VALUING INNOVATION. **I'VE NEVER HAD SUCH POSITIVE FEED BACK** ON ANY GIFT WE'VE GIVEN. PEOPLE JUST KEEP TALKING ABOUT HOW MUCH THEY VALUED THE BOOK AND HOW PERFECTLY IT TIED BACK TO OUR CONFERENCE MESSAGE. — MICHAEL R. MARCEY, EFFICIENT CAPITAL MANAGEMENT, LLC.

THE SMALL INSPIRATIONAL BOOKS BY SIMPLE TRUTHS ARE **AMAZING MAGIC!** THEY SPARK MY SPIRIT AND ENERGIZE MY SOUL. — JEFF HUGHES, UNITED AIRLINES

MR. ANDERSON, EVER SINCE A FRIEND OF MINE SENT ME THE 212 MOVIE ONLINE, **I HAVE BECOME A RAVING FAN** OF SIMPLE TRUTHS. I LOVE AND APPRECIATE THE POSITIVE MESSAGES YOUR PRODUCTS CONVEY AND I HAVE FOUND MANY WAYS TO USE THEM. THANK YOU FOR YOUR VISION. — PATRICK SHAUGHNESSY, AVI COMMUNICATIONS, INC.